the TRUTH *will* MAKE *you* FREE

The Truth Will Make You Free
Copyright © 2022 Deneen Penny-Rymes

All rights reserved.

No part of this publication may be reproduced in a retrieval system, or transmitted in any form or by any means—electronic, mechanical, photocopying, recording, or otherwise—without the prior written permission of the publisher.

This manuscript has undergone viable editorial work and proofreading, yet human limitations may have resulted in minor grammatical or syntax-related errors remaining in the finished book. The understanding of the reader is requested in these cases. While precaution has been taken in the preparation of this book, the publisher and author assume no responsibility for errors or omissions, or for damages resulting from the use of the information contained herein.

This book is set in the typeface *Athelas* designed by Veronika Burian and Jose Scaglione.

Paperback ISBN: 978-1-0880-2661-8

A Publication of *Tall Pine Books*
119 E Center Street, Suite B4A | Warsaw, Indiana 46580
www.tallpinebooks.com

| 1 22 22 20 16 02 |

Published in the United States of America

the TRUTH will MAKE you FREE

a FIFTY-TWO *week* REVELATION JOURNAL

written by
DENEEN PENNY-RYMES

PERSONAL THANK YOU TO:

Eric Gilmore who was so gracious and kind to me. He went out of his way and quickly connected me with his publisher. He is the reason this book is now on shelves.

Samuel A. Wright my dear friend and brother did not hesitate to sow into the production of this book. I am grateful to have such a supportive friend.

My precious cousin **Ashley Nichole Rock-Wylie,** one of the sweetest souls I know. Her benevolence will never be forgotten.

Jackie Dixon, a true sister in Christ, demonstrated her love by believing in this project enough to give so it would be a success.

Karen Staton trusted God enough to support me without really knowing me but trusted the Christ in me.

To **Leon Pickett,** his Christ-like benevolence and belief in this book has been an inspiration and a life changer.

Amelia Jackson, one of my most precious and dearest friends. She is a bright shining light in my life. Her contribution not only helped me but countless others.

A special thanks to all the photographers that so graciously shared their beautiful photos for everyone to enjoy! You have blessed so many.

And my kind, faithful, generous, publisher **Nick Poe**, who has been so patient and thoughtful, and such a man of integrity. I couldn't have asked for a better person to collaborate with. Also, I can't forget the indispensable help from his assistant **Austin Penn.**

...AND THE TRUTH WILL MAKE YOU FREE...

We are evolving into a deeper understanding of who God is. God's Word (the Truth) reveals to us the nature of God, the nature of man, and the nature of our enemy. This revelation empowers us to live a Heavenly Kingdom life here on earth.

"...Your Kingdom come, Your will be done, on earth as it is in Heaven..."
Matthew 6:10

INTRODUCTION

This book is not exhaustive; it was birthed out of my personal life encounters. Not only is this book not exhaustive of the Truth it is also not exhaustive of my life's discoveries about the Truth. This book contains some of the lessons that have rendered me revelation.

I'm no expert, I'm just a contributor in the quest for the "TRUTH". I am not the message I am a messenger. There is no perfect messenger only a perfect message which is the "TRUTH". The definition for perfection is relative. Let's just say perfection in this context means there is no need for improvement, enlightenment, or spiritual awakening. We may not yet be perfect but we are complete. We've been created with everything we need to reach perfection. This life's journey is our process to that goal. The only relevancy is "TRUTH". The "TRUTH" is what makes us free!

I hope my life's lessons enhance your "divine purpose".

SUGGESTED USE *of* THIS BOOK

The ideal way to start this book would be to begin the first week in January of each year. But you can start at the beginning of any week in the year. Just make sure you make note of the day (date) you start so you can keep up with the weekly message.

Read the book in its entirety, then read one message a week and think about it, take notes and pray.

This book can be read and meditated on year after year.

As we mature the revelation will mature.

I pray you will be blessed by these simple yet profound life's lessons. They may be revelation to some but a reminder to others.

Enjoy the book

WEEK ONE

"...and the TRUTH will make you FREE..."

Transparency allows "THE LIGHT" to shine through you.

When we are our authentic selves, we are perfect vessels to help, serve, and display God's goodness in the earth.

WEEKLY NOTES
and PRAYERS

"If we walk in the Light as He is in the Light, we have fellowship with one another." 1 John 1:7

WEEK TWO

"...and the TRUTH will make you FREE..."

God will make your enemy either your footstool or be at peace with you *(Psalm 110:1 & Proverbs 16:7)*

Kindness produces kindness and/or destroys cruelty.

WEEKLY NOTES *and* PRAYERS

"If it is possible, as much as depend on you, live peaceably with all Men." Romans 12:18

_____
_____
_____
_____
_____
_____
_____
_____
_____
_____
_____
_____
_____
_____
_____
_____
_____
_____

WEEK THREE

"...and the TRUTH will make you FREE..."

Until I am totally consumed and embodied with unconditional love I'll be in pursuit.

If we have anything short of love in our hearts, we have not learned all we need to learn. Love is the ultimate goal in life.

WEEKLY NOTES
and PRAYERS

"Beloved, let us love one another, for God is Love, and everyone who loves is born of God and knows God." 1 John 4:7

WEEK FOUR
"...and the TRUTH will make you FREE..."

Be a liberator and become liberated. Oppression is born out of FEAR and IGNORANCE which produces a multiplicity of human enemies, i.e., greed, control, imperialism, entitlement, self-destruction, etc...etc...etc...

Freedom comes when we are free of our <u>need</u> to control and/or dominate people, environments, and circumstances.

WEEKLY NOTES
and PRAYERS

God has not given you a spirit of fear, but of power and of love and a sound mind." 2 Timothy 1:7

"For He who fears has not been made perfect in love." 1 John 4:18ba

___

WEEK FIVE

"...and the TRUTH will make you FREE..."

Take a close look at your beautiful self and embrace you, accept you, love you...God does. We are a reflection of the God of this universe. He made us in His image.

WEEKLY NOTES *and* PRAYERS

"...We have been fearfully and wondrously made..." Psalm 139:14

WEEK SIX

"...and the TRUTH will make you FREE..."

We are more than what is apparent. We are the incarnation of life's complexities.

We should be careful not to judge anything or anybody according to the limited information we have. There's often more to the story than meets the eye.

WEEKLY NOTES
and PREGNANT

"For man sees the outward appearance, but the Lord sees the heart." I Samuel 16:7

_____
_____
_____
_____
_____
_____
_____
_____
_____
_____
_____
_____
_____
_____
_____
_____
_____
_____
_____
_____
_____
_____
_____

WEEK SEVEN

"...and the TRUTH will make you FREE..."

We are all different, yet fit perfectly together to form a perfect union.

Everyone has a particular purpose that cannot be performed by anyone else, and is necessary for the function of the whole community.

WEEKLY NOTES
and PRAYERS

"The body is a unit, though it is made up of many parts, and though all its parts are many, they form one body. So it is with Christ." 2 Corinthians 12:12

WEEK EIGHT
"...and the TRUTH will make you FREE..."

Nothing can satisfy our need except the One who created the need.

As humans we naturally have desires. We sometimes look for satisfaction in people, places and things. Until one day, we find out our insatiable appetites are never satisfied. The only One able to quench that thirst is the God of all creation.

WEEKLY NOTES
and PRAYERS

"All things were made through Him, and without Him nothing was made." John 1:3

WEEK NINE
"...and the TRUTH will make you FREE..."

I refuse to have one dimensional thinking or understanding. I aspire to have an open-mind, to allow unlimited creativity to expand my limited perspectives, so I can experience unlimited possibilities. As we seek enlightenment our perspectives change and open us up for new revelations.

(Tears of joy)

WEEKLY NOTES *and* PRAYERS

"...the eyes of your understanding being enlightened..."Ephesians 1:18

"And now for a little while grace has been shown from the Lord our God, to leave us a remnant to escape, and give us a peg in His holy place, that our God may enlighten our eyes and give us a measure of revival in our bondage." Ezra 9:8

WEEK TEN
"...and the TRUTH will make you FREE..."

Being positive does not mean to pretend there are no problems, difficulties, or challenges in life, or flaws within ourselves. Positive thinking, which manifests positive results, shift our focus to what we want to give power and strength to. It is essential to confront all aspects of our life in order to make the necessary adjustments. We are not freed from negative energy when we ignore the essence of what caused it in the first place. Be true to yourself, be honest, be free!

webs of deception trap us and lead us to destruction

WEEKLY NOTES
and PRAYERS

"For as he thinks in his heart so is he." Proverbs 23:7

WEEK ELEVEN

"...and the TRUTH will make you FREE..."

Be still and listen...we don't know another's truth unless they share it with us...don't judge, what we fear we judge...fear distorts the truth...Be still and listen.

WEEKLY NOTES
and PRAYERS

"He who answers a matter before it is heard, it is folly (a lack of good sense) and shame to him." Proverbs 18:13

WEEK TWELVE

"...and the TRUTH will make you FREE..."

Transparency
There is beauty in transparency, don't hide who you really are. Who you are brings so much to others.

Kindness produces kindness and/or destroys cruelty.

WEEKLY NOTES *and* PRAYERS

"For everything created by God is good, and nothing is to be rejected if it is received with thanksgiving." 1 Timothy 4:4

"For we are God's handiwork, created in Christ Jesus to do good works, which God prepared in advance for us to do." Ephesians 2:10

_____
_____
_____
_____
_____
_____
_____
_____
_____
_____
_____
_____
_____
_____
_____
_____
_____
_____
_____
_____
_____
_____

SOMETHING TO THINK ABOUT

God's gift of Love, Light, Truth, and Life is available to all. The Way to receive His gift is with an open <u>mind</u> and sincere <u>heart</u>.

God is the gift.
He is Love
He is Light
He is the Way
He is the Truth
He is the Life

NOTES *and* PRAYERS

_____
_____
_____
_____
_____
_____
_____
_____
_____
_____
_____
_____
_____

WEEK THIRTEEN
"...and the TRUTH will make you FREE..."

Dogma impairs our ability to receive the truth. When we look at life through a tunnel instead of using our peripheral vision we miss so much.

WEEKLY NOTES *and* PRAYERS

"For the hearts of these people are hardened, and their ears cannot hear, and their eyes cannot see, and their hearts cannot understand, and they cannot turn to Me (God) and let Me heal them. But blessed are your eyes because they see, and your ears because they hear."
Matthew 13:15-16

_____
_____
_____
_____
_____
_____
_____
_____
_____
_____
_____
_____
_____
_____
_____
_____
_____
_____
_____
_____
_____

WEEK FOURTEEN
"...and the TRUTH will make you FREE..."

We must seek the truth to continue to exist. Avoiding the truth may have its temporary comforts but leads to our definite destruction.

WEEKLY NOTES *and* PRAYERS

"My people are destroyed for the lack of knowledge." Hosea 4:6

_____
_____
_____
_____
_____
_____
_____
_____
_____
_____
_____
_____
_____
_____
_____
_____
_____
_____
_____
_____
_____
_____

WEEK FIFTEEN
"...and the TRUTH will make you FREE..."

Be careful declaring something as absolute truth. Our understanding of truth evolves as we mature. a

WEEKLY NOTES *and* PRAYERS

"I have not yet apprehended (know all there is to know); but this one thing I do, forgetting those things which are behind (not let the past hinder my perspective), and reaching forward to those things which are ahead..." Philippians 3:12-13

WEEK SIXTEEN
"...and the TRUTH will make you FREE..."

With guidance people will find their own way. We need not force our believes, thoughts, or experiences on others, just assist and the way will be made clear.

WEEKLY NOTES
and PRAYERS

"...serve as overseers not by compulsion but willingly, eagerly, nor as being lords over those entrusted to you, but being examples..." 1 Peter 5:3

WEEK SEVENTEEN
"...and the TRUTH will make you FREE..."

Avoid allowing our differences to separate us, but rather enjoy, embrace, and understand one another. Those are the things that enrich our lives and make us more enlightened and better human beings.

WEEKLY NOTES *and* PRAYERS

"There is diversity of gifts but the same Spirit. There are differences in ministries but the same Lord, and there is diversity of activities but it is the same God who works in all. But the manifestation of the Spirit is given to each one for the profit of all." 1 Corinthians 12:4-7

WEEK EIGHTEEN
"...and the TRUTH will make you FREE..."

The essence of God is everywhere. The perimeters of God are nowhere. My truth is that God is an all knowing, all powerful, everywhere present being, without boundaries or limits, without beginning or end.

We encounter Truth all the time but we don't always accept it. Truth can be found everywhere and in everything.

WEEKLY NOTES *and* PRAYERS

"But who is able to build Him a temple, since heaven and heaven of heavens cannot contain Him." 2 Chronicles 2:6

_____
_____
_____
_____
_____
_____
_____
_____
_____
_____
_____
_____
_____
_____
_____
_____
_____
_____
_____
_____
_____

WEEK NINETEEN
"...and the TRUTH will make you FREE..."

Be-Attitude
"Beatitudes"

Be your attitude. Our attitude will determine what we will be. If our core attitude and perspective towards life and people are skewed then we will experience massacre after massacre in the form of devasted relationships, failed expectations, and broken dreams. Yet when we display beauty from the inside, i.e., forgiveness, tolerance, encouragement, our outside reflects an attractive brightness.

WEEKLY NOTES
and PRAYERS

Blessed are the Merciful, thoughtful, kind, for they will receive the same. (Paraphrased from Matthew 5:7)

_____
_____
_____
_____
_____
_____
_____
_____
_____
_____
_____
_____
_____
_____
_____
_____
_____
_____
_____
_____
_____

WEEK TWENTY

"...and the TRUTH will make you FREE..."

We don't know joy because we have not experienced tribulation, but because of it.

WEEKLY NOTES
and PREFERS

WEEKLY NOTES
and PRAYERS

"If we walk in the Light as He is in the Light, we have fellowship with one another." 1 John 1:7

WEEK TWENTY-ONE
"...and the TRUTH will make you FREE..."

EMBRACE – ENGAGE – EXECUTE
Embrace God's love Engage in self love
Execute by giving love to others

WEEKLY NOTES
and PRAYERS

"You shall love Your <u>God</u> with all your heart, with all your soul, with all your mind, this is the first and great commandment, and the second is like it: "You shall love your <u>neighbor</u> as <u>yourself</u>." Matthew 22:37-39

WEEK TWENTY-TWO
"...and the TRUTH will make you FREE..."

EMBRACE – ENGAGE – EXECUTE
Embrace the Light
Engage the Truth
Execute your Divine Purpose

WEEKLY NOTES
and PRAYERS

God is Light and in Him is no darkness at all. If we say that we have fellowship with Him, and walk in darkness, we lie and do not practice the Truth." 1 John 1:5-6

WEEK TWENTY-THREE
"...and the TRUTH will make you FREE..."

I rather be loathed for who I am than loved for who I am not.

A quote I read somewhere, "I'd rather be known as a honest sinner than as a lying hypocrite" *(Unknown author)*

WEEKLY NOTES
and PRAYERS

"...even so you also appear righteous to men, but inside you are full of hypocrisy and lawlessness." Matthew 23:28

WEEK TWENTY-FOUR
"...and the TRUTH will make you FREE..."

I don't believe intelligence is equated to our ability to memorize information. I believe we become intellectually astute when we are open to learn and explore.

WEEKLY NOTES *and* PRAYERS

"Study to show yourselves approved to God, a worker who does not need to be ashamed, rightly dividing the word of truth." 2 Timothy 2:15

_____
_____
_____
_____
_____
_____
_____
_____
_____
_____
_____
_____
_____
_____
_____
_____
_____
_____
_____
_____

WEEK TWENTY-FIVE
"...and the TRUTH will make you FREE..."

When we feel the need to dominate others it's because we are afraid.

Aggression camouflages fear

WEEKLY NOTES
and PRAYERS

"What the wicked fear will come upon them, but the desires of the righteous will be given to them." Proverbs 10:24

WEEK TWENTY-SIX

"...and the TRUTH will make you FREE..."

An oppressor is one disguising weakness as strength. True power is gentle.

WEEKLY NOTES
and PREYERS

"...who being in the form of God did not consider it robbery to be equal with God, but made Himself of no reputation, taking on the form of a bondservant and coming in the form of men. And being found in appearance as a man, He humbled Himself and became obedient to the point of death, even the death of the cross." Philippians 2:6-8

WEEK TWENTY-SEVEN
"...and the TRUTH will make you FREE..."

Transparency

Our authentic self is not what we possess, the work we do, our abilities, or our social status. Who we really are can't be seen or measured, we just simply are enough.

WEEKLY NOTES *and* PRAYERS

"Take heed and beware of covetousness, for one's life does not consist in the abundance of the things he possesses." Luke 12:15

WEEK TWENTY-EIGHT

"...and the TRUTH will make you FREE..."

When we feel the need to be right or proof our point, it's because we identify who we are with what we know or do. Who we really are is not a contest of wit or skill, whatever we contribute is valuable, we are simply enough.

Kindness produces kindness and/or destroys cruelty.

WEEKLY NOTES
and PRAYERS

"For I'm confident of this very thing, that He who began a good work in you will perfect (complete) it until the day of Jesus Christ." Philippians 1:6

_____
_____
_____
_____
_____
_____
_____
_____
_____
_____
_____
_____
_____
_____
_____
_____
_____
_____
_____
_____
_____

WEEK TWENTY-NINE
"...and the TRUTH will make you FREE..."

Transparency

The knowledge we have obtained, our education we have achieved, our physical appearance we've worked so hard to acquire, who we know, our family lineage, our belief systems, our nationality, race, or religion, none of these things are who we are. We are not the sum total of external temporal things, we are eternal beings, and we are simply enough.

WEEKLY NOTES *and* PRAYERS

"...while we do not look at the things which are seen, but at the things which are not seen. For the things which are seen are temporary, but the things which are not seen are eternal." 2 Corinthians 4:18

_____
_____
_____
_____
_____
_____
_____
_____
_____
_____
_____
_____
_____
_____
_____
_____
_____
_____
_____
_____
_____
_____

WEEK THIRTY
"...and the TRUTH will make you FREE..."

Transparency

When we allow external temporal things to become our identity, we become <u>dependent</u> on those things to make us whole and complete. Without those THINGS we can begin to feel a deep-seated sense of lack, incompleteness, and emptiness. We have been created with everything we need to be whole, complete, and to fulfill our divine purpose; we simply are enough. When we become grateful for who we are right now our worth barometer starts to rise. We are simply enough.

WEEKLY NOTES
and PRAYERS

"Don't lay up for yourself treasures on earth, where moth and rust destroy and thieves break in and steal. But lay up for yourselves treasures in heaven, where neither moth nor rust destroy and where thieves do not break in and steal." Matthew 6:19

_____

_____
_____
_____
_____
_____
_____
_____
_____
_____
_____
_____
_____
_____
_____
_____
_____
_____
_____
_____
_____
_____

_____

WEEK THIRTY-ONE
"...and the TRUTH will make you FREE..."

Fear can only manifest when we are self-conscience and lacking love. When we direct our attention to the Lord, fear no longer exist.

Faith and love over-powers Fear

WEEKLY NOTES
and PRAYERS

"There is no fear in love, but perfect love casts out all fear."
1 John 4:18

WEEK THIRTY-TWO
"...and the TRUTH will make you FREE..."

Transparency

I have found that too many people have no idea of their value. Not knowing one's value is dangerous to self and others. This lack of understanding causes covetousness, prejudice, envy, jealousy, hatred, strive, and the like...

WEEKLY NOTES
and PRAYERS

"Are not five sparrows sold for two copper coins? Not one of them are forgotten by God. But the very hairs of your head are all numbered. Do not fear, therefore, you are of more value than many sparrows." Luke 12:6-7

WEEK THIRTY-THREE
"...and the TRUTH will make you FREE..."

Transparency

Some things in life are difficult. We learn and we grow when we push through seemingly unbearable situations. And we receive the most wonderful blessings when we endure the discomfort of pressure.

WEEKLY NOTES *and* PRAYERS

"It is good for me that I have been afflicted, that I may learn Your (God's) statutes" Psalms 119:71

WEEK THIRTY-FOUR
"...and the TRUTH will make you FREE..."

It is wise to be <u>transparent</u>. Our true beauty is showcased and the chains of secrecy and dishonesty are broken. Be yourself, be free!!!

WEEKLY NOTES *and* PRAYERS

"Behold, the Lord desires truth in the inward parts, and in the hidden part He will make us to know wisdom." Psalm 51:6

WEEK THIRTY-FIVE
"...and the TRUTH will make you FREE..."

A life separated from God is substituted with EGO (easing God out). The ego creates a false sense of self. We become a branch cut from the vine. The egos' needs are endless. It feels vulnerable and threatened so it lives in a continuous state of fear and want. Connection with our life source empowers us and rids us of want and anxiety. We become assured, safe, and fearless.

WEEKLY NOTES
and PRAYERS

"Do not cast me away from your presence, and do not take Your Holy Spirit from me. Restore to me the joy of your salvation, and uphold me by your generous Spirit." Psalm 51:11-12

WEEK THIRTY-SIX
"...and the TRUTH will make you FREE..."

There are many levels of conscientiousness...God meets us according to where our level of comprehension is, He knows us completely. We see God and all things through the lens of our personal encounters and experiences.

WEEKLY NOTES *and* PRAYERS

"O Lord, You have searched me and know me. You know my sitting down and my rising up; You understand my thought afar off. You comprehend my path and my lying down. And are acquainted with all my ways. For there is not a word on my tongue, But behold, O Lord, You know it altogether." Psalm 139:1-4

WEEK THIRTY-SEVEN
"...and the TRUTH will make you FREE..."

We can <u>Be</u>come wise or we can <u>Be</u>come wounded by things that happen to us.

<u>It's our choice</u>

WEEKLY NOTES
and PRAYERS

"Choose this day whom you will serve, whether the gods of your ancestors...or the gods of the Amorites in whose land you are living (a place of wounds); but as for me and my household (a place of wisdom), we will serve the Lord." Joshua 24:15

WEEK THIRTY-EIGHT
"...and the TRUTH will make you FREE..."

An awakening change and expands our view of who we really are and the world around us. This is essential to evolve and grow.

WEEKLY NOTES
and PRAYERS

"The fear of the Lord is the beginning of wisdom (awakening), and the knowledge of the Holy One is understanding (spiritual growth). Proverbs 9:10

WEEK THIRTY-NINE
"...and the TRUTH will make you FREE..."

Be-Attitude

The goal is to press towards being Love not doing loving acts. When we do something or perform an act, it's changeable. But when we Be-come something, we are that thing, and that will always Be. Don't just show love Be love. For example, we can gallop, and we can cease from galloping. But if we are a horse (figuratively speaking) whether we gallop or not we are still a horse. We never cease from being a horse. So it is in Be-coming Love. God is Love and God is Truth. Let us aspire to <u>Be</u> more like our creator.

WEEKLY NOTES *and* PRAYERS

Beatitude

"Blessed are the pure in heart for they shall see God" Matthew 5:8

WEEK FORTY
"...and the TRUTH will make you FREE..."

God has different relationships and ways of communicating with us all. Some he talks to, some He inspires. We cannot think that the way He deals with one is the way He deals with all. We experience God differently.

WEEKLY NOTES *and* PRAYERS

"...Fear not, for I have redeemed you; I have called you by your name"
Isaiah 43:1

WEEK FORTY-ONE

"...and the TRUTH will make you FREE..."

Our entire being needs our attention (body, mind/soul, and spirit) for us to be healthy and well balanced. The lack of attention to any one part prevents us from fulfilling our full potential.

WEEKLY NOTES *and* PRAYERS

"Beloved, I pray that you may prosper in all things and be in good health just as your soul prospers." 3 John 1:2

WEEK FORTY-TWO
"...and the TRUTH will make you FREE..."

Restoration for Impartation
<u>We can only give what we have in our possession</u>

We can't feed others when we're still hunger.
We need to be fed before we can feed.

We can't teach when our information has not yet been experienced.
We must first be taught (experientially) before we are eligible to teach.

We can't lead when we can barely walk without falling.
We learn to lead by being a humble/submissive follower. In other words, we need to be led before we can be an effective leader.

WEEKLY NOTES
and PRAYERS

"Restore to me the joy of Your salvation, and uphold me by Your free Spirit. Then I will teach transgressors Your ways, and sinners shall be converted to You." Psalm 51:12-13

WEEK FORTY-THREE
"...and the TRUTH will make you FREE..."

Humility

It is a blessing to be used...not abused

Think about it this way...when we're <u>used</u>, we are not <u>useless</u>. We are called to be broken bread and poured out wine. Just as Christ is our living sacrifice.

WEEKLY NOTES
and PRAYERS

"And being found in appearance as a man. He humbled Himself and became obedient to the point of death, even the death of the cross." Philippians 2:8

WEEK FORTY-FOUR
"...and the TRUTH will make you FREE..."

Anything stolen whether it be physical, mental, or spiritual, doesn't promote prosperity, it produces despair and poverty.

WEEKLY NOTES
and PRAYERS

Jesus said, "The thieve does not come except to kill, steal, and to destroy. I have come that they may have life, and that they have it more abundantly." John 10:10

_____
_____
_____
_____
_____
_____
_____
_____
_____
_____
_____
_____
_____
_____
_____
_____
_____
_____
_____
_____
_____
_____
_____

WEEK FORTY-FIVE
"...and the TRUTH will make you FREE..."

Fear produces unrest within which manifest discord without.

WEEKLY NOTES
and PRAYERS

"There is no fear in love; perfect love cast out all fear, because fear involves torment." 1 John 4:18

WEEK FORTY-SIX
"...and the TRUTH will make you FREE..."

The more we reach for things on the outside of us to make us rich, the more it reveals the bankruptcy on the inside of us that makes us poor.

WEEKLY NOTES
and PRAYERS

"Seek first the Kingdom of God and His righteousness, and all these things will be added to you." Matthew 6:33

WEEK FORTY-SEVEN

"...and the TRUTH will make you FREE..."

Beautiful things are made when we work together.

WEEKLY NOTES *and* PRAYERS

"Behold, how good and pleasant it is for brethren to dwell together in unity." Psalm 133:1

WEEK FORTY-EIGHT
"...and the TRUTH will make you FREE..."

My perception determines if I live in peace or despair.

WEEKLY NOTES
and PRAYERS

"Finally, brethren, whatever things are true, whatever things are noble, whatever things are just, whatever things are lovely, whatever things are of good report, if there is any virtue and if there is anything praiseworthy-meditate on these things." Philippians 4:8

WEEK FORTY-NINE
"...and the TRUTH will make you FREE..."

Society conditions us to always be first or better than someone else, in some situations at their expense. Why are some people motivated by the distress of others? Our self-esteem should not be based on the misfortune of another. That does not make us superior.

Life is not a competition

Life is a privilege

Life is an experience

We all have something to contribute of value. None of us is great at everything. The one who desires to be superior is the one that does not value their own worth. We can strive to be excellent without aspiring to be superior. We should always aspire to produce quality of that which we've been created to be.

Whether we're first or last we can still be a relevant contributor. We all have value.

WEEKLY NOTES
and PRAYERS

Jesus said, "The first shall be last and the last shall be first" (Matthew 20:16)

WEEK FIFTY
"...and the TRUTH will make you FREE..."

My value is not based on your acknowledgement of my significance. I'm valuable because I'm valuable.

WEEKLY NOTES *and* PRAYERS

"For there is no partiality with God." Romans 2:11

"...In truth I perceive that God shows no partiality." Acts 10:34b

WEEK FIFTY-ONE
"...and the TRUTH will make you FREE..."

Fear and ignorance are man's biggest enemy. The lack of love is its origin.

WEEKLY NOTES
and PRAYERS

"For he who fears has not been made perfect in love." 1 John 4:18b

WEEK FIFTY-TWO
"...and the TRUTH will make you FREE..."

Whatever we <u>are</u> we reproduce. We reproduce in serveral ways; biological, socially, emotionally, and spiritually. So let us be mindful of what and who we <u>are</u>, because we impact the world by that choice.

WEEKLY NOTES *and* PRAYERS

"God created man in His own image; in the image of God He created male and female He created them. Then God blessed them, and God said be fruitful and multiply..." Genesis 1:27,28A

_____
_____
_____
_____
_____
_____
_____
_____
_____
_____
_____
_____
_____
_____
_____
_____
_____
_____
_____

SOMETHING TO THINK ABOUT
"...and the TRUTH will make you FREE..."

The Truth only provides liberty when we invest quality time learning WHO and what Truth is. Jesus said "I Am
The WAY, I AM The TRUTH, I Am The LIFE..."

When we get to know Him we learn The TRUTH and that spiritual awakening emancipates us.

As we learn of Him we learn He is pure LOVE and that LOVE is poured on, in, and through us without measure.

I discovered, "To know Him is to love Him, to love Him is to trust Him, to trust Him is to obey Him.

Obeying Him is simply adhering to Universal principles/laws that God has established in the earth to keep us safe and bless our lives. These Principles parallel the government of His Heavenly Kingdom.

If this book has blessed you in any way, <u>share it with others</u>, <u>give it as a gift</u>. We have all been given something to give to others. I pray that what our Heavenly Father has revealed to me will enhance your life's journey as you pursue a deeper substantive relationship with Him.

May you have a life enriched with abundant blessings!

SOMETHING TO THINK ABOUT

(Sharing an intimate part of me with you)

There is nothing I desire more than to know God.
The biblical meaning of the word "know" infers intimacy.
Intimacy is the closeness we share with someone else.

The more I get to know our Heavenly Father, the more I crave Him. I've come to know Him as a sweetness that is addictive. The Bible describe God (His Word) as being sweeter than honey to my mouth!
(Psalm 119:103)
To <u>know</u> Him

To <u>understand</u> His ways

To share an active role in the <u>wisdom</u> He imparts to all who seek Him with their whole heart.

To become so enmeshed with Him that I am effortlessly identified with Him.

To live in His presence, where all that I long for exist.

This is my greatest desire; this <u>truth makes me free</u>.

"Yet indeed I count all things loss for the excellence of the knowledge of <u>Christ Jesus my Lord</u>...that I may know Him and the power of His resurrection, and the fellowship of His suffering, being conformed to His death..." Philippians 3:8a, 10

AUTHOR'S PERSONAL TRUTH

Deneen believes in being still enough to hear from God, yet serving enough not to be idle. She strives to be open-minded and non-judgmental, looking with peripheral vision not tunnel vision. As she journeys through life her experiences have taught her to use comas not periods because she knows her repertoire of knowledge is not exhaustive. She embraces the universe as her classroom and identifies herself as an eternal student

She has authored and has been a contributing author to several books, including an autobiography called "What The Devil Meant For Evil, God Meant For Good", "God's Perfect Order", "Life Happens But We Can Finish", and several other Publication.

Apostle Dee operates in the apostolic, prophetic, teaching, healing, and exhortation ministries charged to build up **leaders** and empower the body of Christ. She fashions her appointed ministry after: Isaiah 61:1-2 and Luke 18-19, *"The Spirit of the Lord is upon me, to preach the gospel to the poor; He has sent me to heal the broken hearted. To proclaim liberty to the captives and recovery of sight to the blind. To set at liberty those who are oppressed; To proclaim the acceptable year of the Lord."*

www.ingramcontent.com/pod-product-compliance
Lightning Source LLC
Chambersburg PA
CBHW041503010526
44118CB00001B/8